WHAT WERE CHESTER NEZ'S SECRET CODES?

WRITTEN BY:
CATHY WERLING
& SILVIA MIRANDA

ILLUSTRATED BY:
CHRISTINA MALICKE

PUBLISHED BY:

© 2025 LOWELL MILKEN CENTER FOR UNSUNG HEROES
ALL RIGHTS RESERVED

During computer class, Latham Nez listened as his teacher explained how codes help computers communicate. She explained that computer codes are like secret languages understood only by computers. After teaching them about these codes, the teacher said they would work in teams to create their own code to produce a simple computer game.

Latham was excited about the coding project and hoped his friends, Benny Catron and Veronica Madrid, would be his partners. On their walk home after school, Latham learned that his friends weren't thrilled about the project. Veronica said, "Why do we have to learn a code that only computers understand?"

As Benny agreed, Latham said, "You guys, we can talk to computers using this code and program them to do things for us. This can change our lives!"

They had already planned to go to Latham's house after school, so he thought it would be a perfect opportunity for his dad to share something with them about codes. When the kids arrived, Latham's dad, Michael Nez, was in his art studio. They grabbed a snack and headed to the studio, where Latham told his dad about the computer code project.

Latham asked his dad to share stories about how his father, Chester Nez (Latham's grandfather), used a special code to change the lives of millions of people. At first, Latham's friends weren't too sure about listening to a story involving a code used long ago, but as Chester's story unfolded, their eyes lit up, eager to learn more.

Michael told them that his father's most famous experience with codes was as a Navajo Code Talker during World War II. "However," he said, "my dad's path to being a Code Talker started much earlier. Growing up as a proud member of the Navajo Nation and living on the Navajo Reservation within New Mexico and Arizona taught him many important codes for his life."

"Starting at the age of five, my father, whose Navajo name was Betoli, helped herd his family's sheep, often walking 15 miles a day," said Latham's dad. "He and his family lived with the sheep, protecting them from coyotes and other dangers. This made Betoli unafraid of hard work and kept him in great physical shape."

"Navajo children were taught to respect others and to respect nature. The entire family cooperated in caring for each other and their livestock, always coming together to help one another. He always remembered his family's words, 'To live in nature is to walk in beauty.' Betoli's love for his family, baby goats, and prairie dog pets helped him show kindness and strength through positive relationships."

"Because Navajo was only a spoken language and not written, Betoli and the other children developed a keen ability to memorize. It was a difficult language, requiring children to think about what they wanted to say before saying it correctly. This helped develop the Navajo people's strong reasoning ability and intelligence."

"Hózhóogo naasháa doo"
I walk in beauty

"In years past, the government had caused hard times for the Navajo people, including forcing them to leave their land for many years and later causing the death of many of their herds of animals. Some departments of the U.S. government wanted the Navajo people to forget their traditions, especially their language, and learn to speak English. When Betoli was eight and sent to a boarding school, a missionary suggested he not use his Navajo name but instead tell the teachers his name was Chester. Those in charge of the school shaved off his hair and only allowed him to speak English, a language he hadn't yet learned."

"Chester had tough days at boarding school, but he was determined to show the courage and patience he had learned growing up. He stood strong even when the teachers washed his mouth with soap because he spoke Navajo words or hit him on the head for breaking a rule he didn't understand. Chester remembered how his family had cared for him, as he comforted his younger sister and the other Navajo children who cried because they had little food, no warmth, and no kindness."

"My dad, Chester, could not wait for the summers when he would return to his family on their precious land, herd sheep and goats, and speak his native Navajo language with the people he loved. He treasured every moment, especially the evenings under the stars when he could catch up on his ancestors' stories, learning his people's sacred traditions which forever bound them together and could never be taken away."

"Every fall, Chester returned to boarding school, and as an eighth grader, he graduated from his first school, Fort Defiance. He attended two other schools, requiring him to live away from home each school year. When Chester was at the boarding school in Tuba City, the principal called together all the young Navajo men to hear the announcement that America had entered World War II."

"There had been an attack by the Japanese on American soil at Pearl Harbor, and America was entering the war to defend our country. Chester and his Navajo friends had been born to be warriors for their people. They saw themselves as part of the earth they lived on, eager to serve and defend their motherland and their families."

"Several months after war was declared, Marine recruiters came to Chester's school, announcing that they needed young Navajo men who spoke both excellent English and Navajo. These young Navajos would be tested to see if they qualified for the Marines' special secret project. They would have to pass basic training before learning their secret assignment."

"After successfully passing both basic training and his Marine interview, while demonstrating his ability to speak excellent English and Navajo, Chester learned that he was among the first 29 Navajo men chosen for a special project to create a secret code using the Navajo language. Because the Japanese enemies had figured out every code sent by Americans over the radios, there needed to be a new code that could not be broken. The Navajo language was suggested as the key to creating that code."

"After finishing basic training in the Marines, Chester and the other 28 new Navajo Marines were locked in a room to create an unbreakable code. Their language was never written, so it would be impossible for non-Navajos to understand or speak it. Except for meal breaks and sleeping, they kept at their work, developing an alphabet using Navajo words for the English letters. The word "cat" in English starts with the letter C. The Navajo word for "cat" was "moasi" (mo-see). So, they used the word "mo-see" to mean the letter C. They also used Navajo words to stand for military terms, locations, and other important words needed in battle."

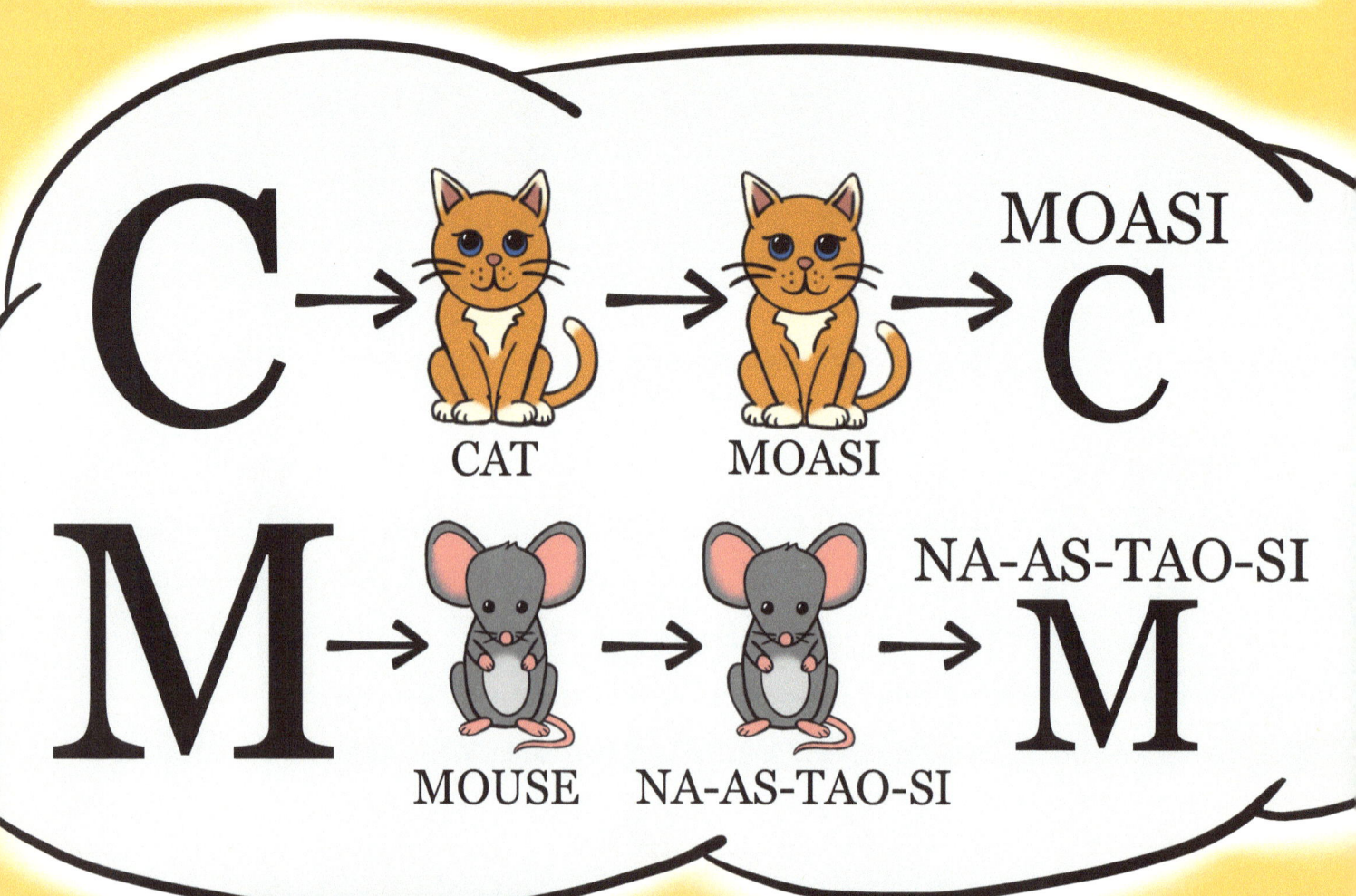

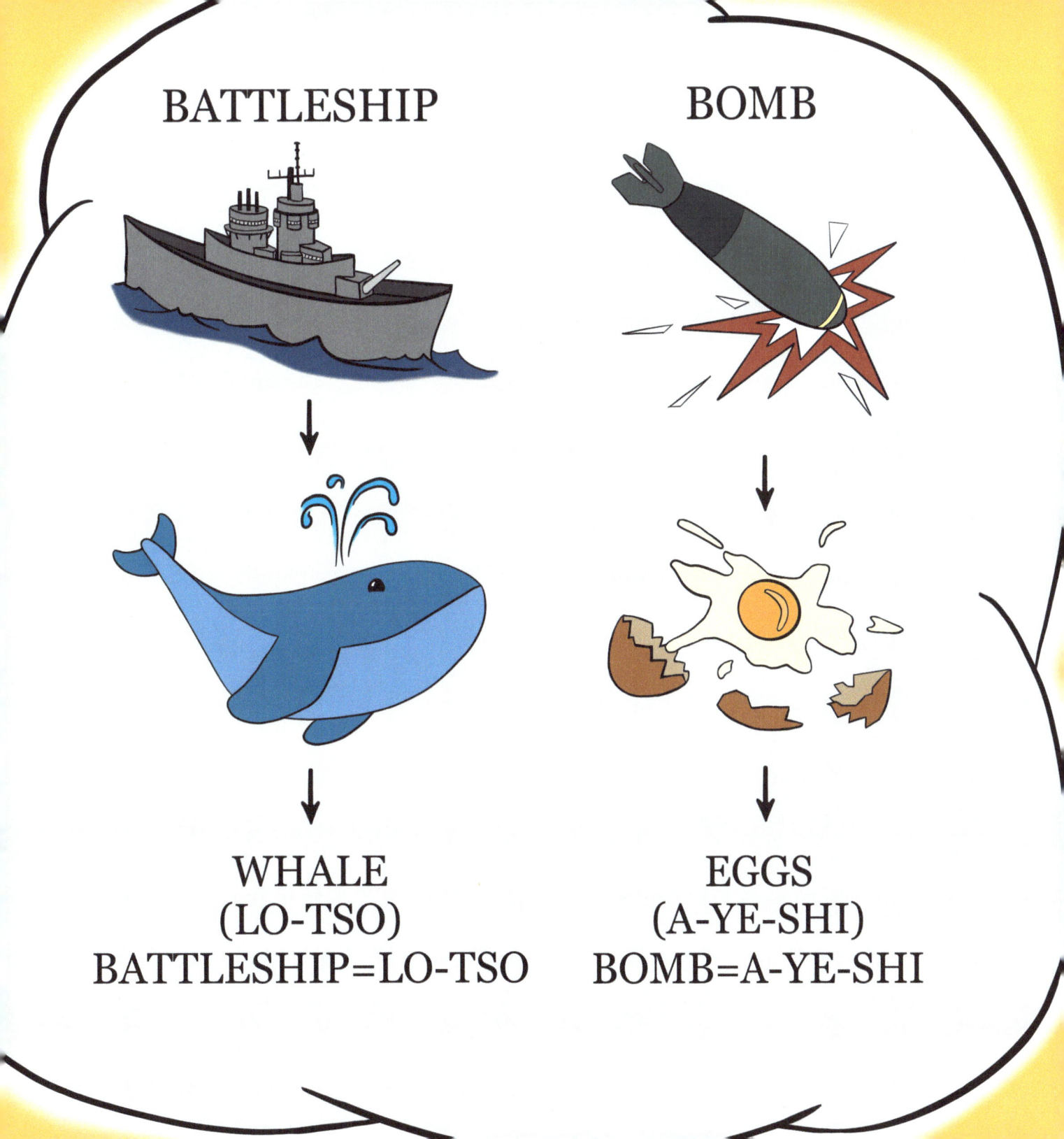

"Their code was tested by expert code breakers who could not figure it out. The code was strong, and the Navajo Marines could send and receive messages in less than three minutes. They were ordered to keep the code secret, with only commanders and officers knowing about it. Chester and the Navajo Code Talkers were then shipped to the Pacific battlefield to begin using the code."

"The code talkers translated important messages into the Navajo code, sending them to other code talkers who decoded them. Working in pairs, they memorized everything without using code books so the enemy couldn't learn the code. The noise of guns and grenades was so loud at times they could barely think, speak, or hear each other. At night or during times with no action, they had to be very quiet so their voices or the squawk of the radio would not give them away."

"They sent messages day and night, telling where US planes and ships should land or fire, where the enemy was located, where more troops were needed, or where to pick up injured soldiers. Short messages could be sent and received in as little as 20 seconds. During one major battle, they successfully sent over 800 messages without a single mistake! Their work was important, yet stressful, as they had to keep themselves safe through the action."

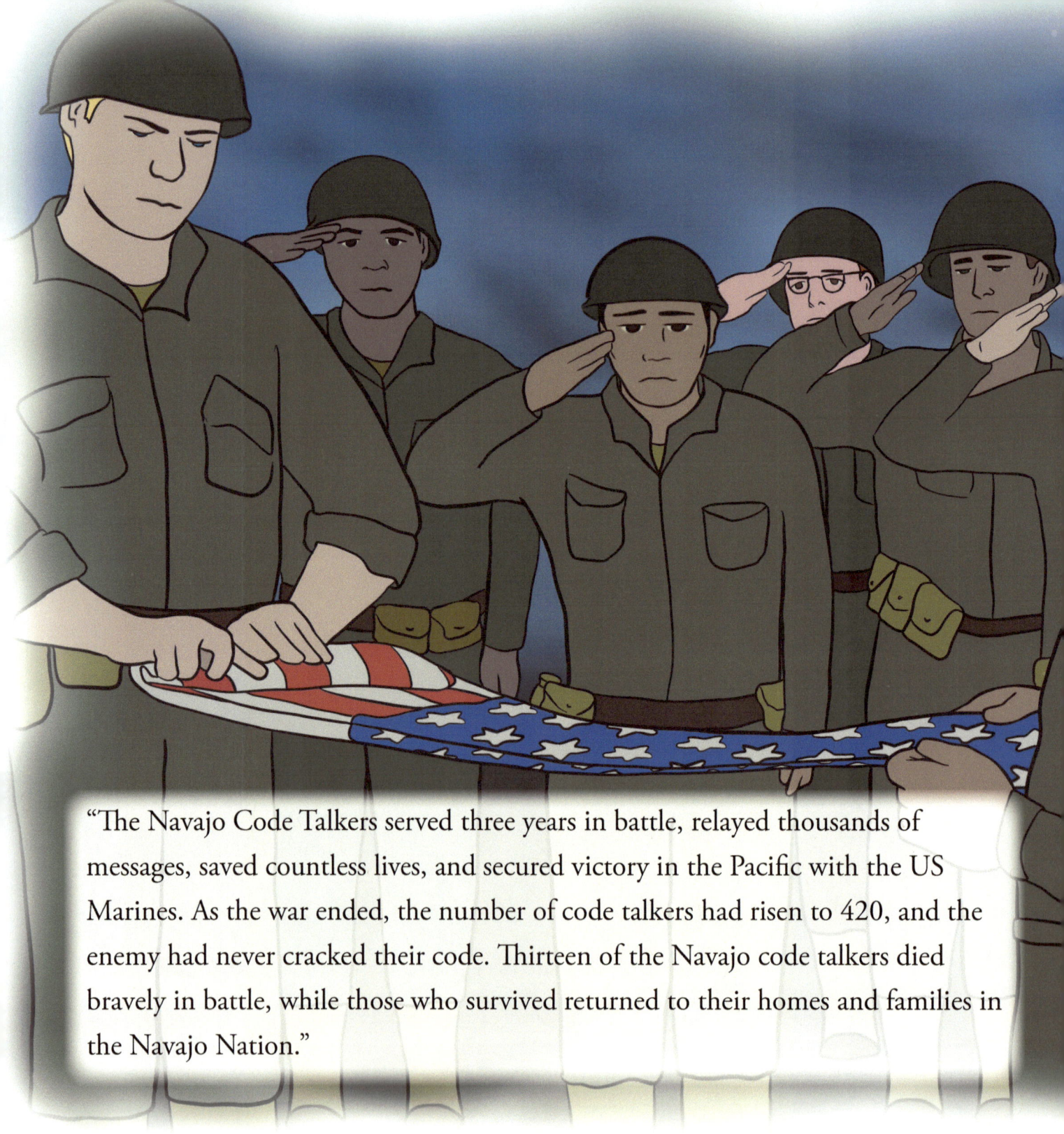

"The Navajo Code Talkers served three years in battle, relayed thousands of messages, saved countless lives, and secured victory in the Pacific with the US Marines. As the war ended, the number of code talkers had risen to 420, and the enemy had never cracked their code. Thirteen of the Navajo code talkers died bravely in battle, while those who survived returned to their homes and families in the Navajo Nation."

"While the critical role of Chester and the other code talkers during WWII remained classified for over 20 years after the war, these unsung heroes were dealing with hard memories of their years during battle. Chester found healing and peace again by returning to live among his Navajo family and friends."

"The code using their language had been his focus during the war, but the other codes of life Chester learned as a child were the ones that gave him strength during wartime. The cooperation and kindness that were part of his life and responsibility in a Navajo family helped him work patiently and respectfully with his fellow soldiers. Because his Navajo language was never written down until many years after the war, Chester's abilities to memorize, reason, and understand were very strong."

"During the war, Chester needed the courage and determination he learned during dangerous times as a sheep herder or hurtful times at boarding school. Caring for animals and living in nature with his fellow Navajos gave him a code of respect for life and the earth on which he lived, leading him to want to do all he could to defend his home and country."

As Michael finished his story, Latham looked at his dad and said thoughtfully, "The code Grandpa used wasn't just about sending messages, was it? It was more than secret words and letters."

"Exactly!" Michael said. "Your grandpa lived by the values he learned as a child and stayed true to those values, just as he stayed true to his language and culture. His strength didn't come from the language code he used in the war, but from the life code he lived every day. Coding is about creating something that can help others, just like the code Chester helped create. As you create the code for your game, it's important to think about the kind of message you want to send."

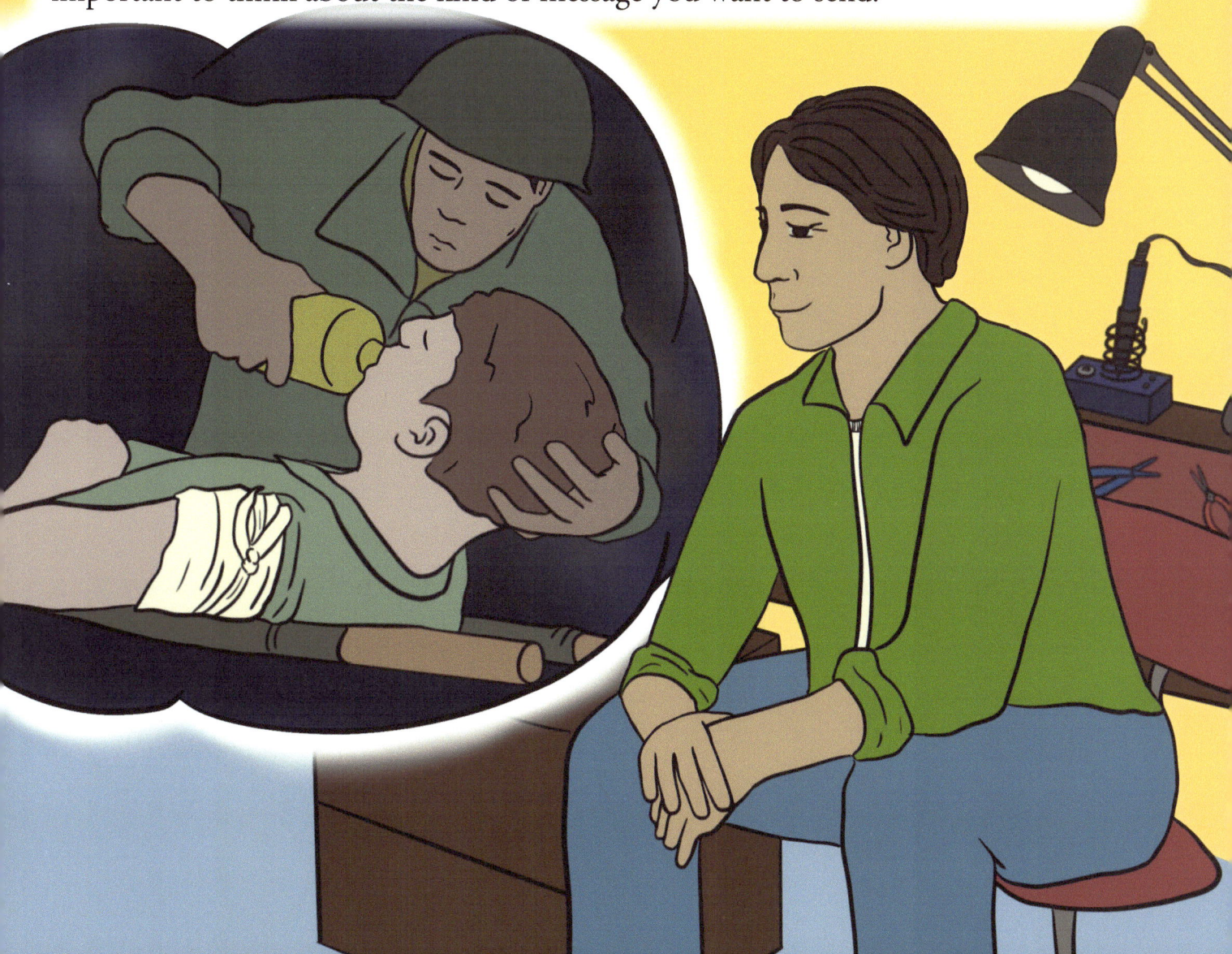

Then Veronica's face lit up. "What if we create a game where players solve puzzles using code words that stand for good character traits, like honesty and courage?"

"Yeah!" Benny agreed. "The more positive traits they collect, the stronger their character becomes in the game."

Latham grinned. "I like it! We could even use some words from the Navajo language like the Code Talkers did. Different levels could represent challenges we might face in life, like the challenges my grandpa Chester faced!"

Mr. Nez beamed with pride. "I know just the word you could use for your title – *Ho'zho'*. It is a Navajo word I often heard in my family. It was a word telling us that in every situation, things would be okay, and beauty, peace, joy, hope, and healing would abound."

Inspired by Chester Nez's story, Latham, Veronica, and Benny worked together to create *Ho'zho*, a game that taught coding and shared the values of a true hero. Their game, filled with secret words and strong life messages, became a favorite in their class, reminding everyone that the best codes are the ones that make the world a better place.

More About Chester Nez

Some Members of Chester's Family in 2011
(Front row) granddaughter Shawnia Nez Whitfield, Chester, and Rita Nez (Michael's wife)
(Back row) grandson Michael Nez, great-grandson Emery Whitfield, grandson Latham Nez, and son Michael Nez
NOTE: Chester's grandson, Latham Nez, and his son, Michael Nez, are the characters in *What Were the Secret Codes of Chester Nez?*

Latham Nez has known Benny Catron and Veronica Madrid since childhood. Benny is his cousin and a good friend, and Veronica is a long-time close friend from his school days.

Chester was one of the original 29 Code Talkers who helped to develop the Navajo Code used in WWII. (He is the first Marine on the second row.)

Chester was the last one of the original 29 members to pass away. He was 93 years old.

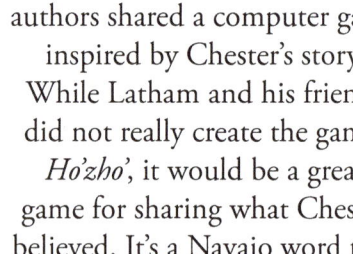

Will you choose to share the values of a hero?

At the end of the book, the authors shared a computer game inspired by Chester's story. While Latham and his friends did not really create the game, *Ho'zho'*, it would be a great game for sharing what Chester believed. It's a Navajo word that reflects peace, beauty, hope, and harmony -- the best things life can offer, even in difficult times.

Chester received his college degree at the University of Kansas, many years after his government money ran out during his last year of college.

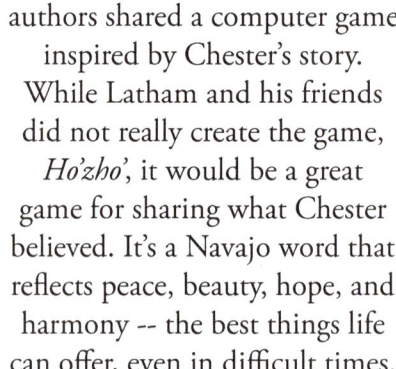

Chester received the Congressional Gold Medal of Honor and had a special celebration given by his Navajo family in New Mexico.

Scan this QR code to try out the game.

Author Cathy Werling is a retired award-winning elementary educator from Fort Scott, Kansas. Her passion for helping students develop positive character traits by seeking out worthy role models led to her work at the Lowell Milken Center for Unsung Heroes. In the fifth book of her Children's Unsung Heroes Book series, *What Were Chester Nez's Secret Codes?* Cathy collaborated with elementary teacher and LMC Fellow Silvia Miranda to share the story of Navajo Code Talker Chester Nez. Through conversations with Chester's family and Judy Avila, the author of his memoir, Cathy learned that Chester's personal "codes for life" exemplified the essential traits that fueled his success as a WWII Code Talker and guided him through many difficult times in his life.

Co-Author Silvia Miranda is a passionate 5th-grade teacher, recognized as a 2018 New Mexico Milken Educator and a 2019 Lowell Milken Center Fellow. In her classroom, she highlights the importance of unsung heroes, particularly those from diverse and minority backgrounds. Silvia believes that children thrive when they see themselves reflected in the stories of those who made meaningful contributions to the world. She gained insight into the legacy of Navajo Code Talker Chester Nez through interviews with his son, Michael, and grandson, Latham. Chester's story comes to life for her students through presentations and discussions highlighting the impact of Chester's heroism. Students are encouraged to explore the lives of heroes from diverse backgrounds, such as Chester's, to develop their unsung hero projects.

Illustrator Christina Malicke is an award-winning professional artist and native Kansan. While her career is in the graphic arts, her works have spanned many mediums - her favorites being drawing and painting. Christina finds joy in using her talents toward positive impacts in her community and beyond. After hearing Chester Nez's story, she felt honored to help further share it with others. She states: "Chester was not only a Navajo Code Talker, but a person of immense character. He reminds us that when we are true to ourselves, strength and perseverance will shine through." Christina strives to continue taking each opportunity to make a difference through her love of art, and to foster the connections that it brings forth.

www.ingramcontent.com/pod-product-compliance
Lightning Source LLC
Chambersburg PA
CBHW041119070526
44584CB00002B/219